God's Little Messengers

Written by: William Parks

Illustrated by: Krystal Parks

AuthorHouse™
1663 Liberty Drive, Suite 200
Bloomington, IN 47403
www.authorhouse.com
Phone: 1-800-839-8640

First published by AuthorHouse 3/16/2009

ISBN: 978-1-4343-6113-4 (sc)

Library of Congress Control Number: 2008900222

Printed in the United States of America
Bloomington, Indiana

This book is printed on acid-free paper.

authorHOUSE®

This book is dedicated to God's Little Messengers who Share the Good News of Jesus Christ with others.

Acknowledgements:

Thank you to Quin Wilder for inspiring me to write this book for children to share Christ with other children.

After several attempts to acquire illustrations for the book from other artists, the Lord provided the unique illustrations in this book through our daughter-in-law, Krystal Parks.

Do you have Jesus in your heart?

Who is Jesus?

How did Jesus save me?

He came from Heaven to Earth as a baby and
grew up in his home helping his parents,
just like you help your parents.

Have you ever been bad
or done something wrong
like steal, lie, been angry
or hurt someone?

Hmmm. Yes,
I did once!

Well, that is called sin.
Jesus came to take our sin away.

How did He take my sin away?

Jesus was punished for the bad things we do by dying on the cross so we could become part of God's Family.

Because Jesus was never bad he went back to
Heaven and if we believe in Him
we can go to Heaven too!

How can I go to Heaven and be with Jesus?

Just ask Him to come into your heart!

Printed in the United States
151195LV00005B